CW01159684

Banbury
in old picture postcards volume 2

by Brian Little

European Library ZALTBOMMEL/THE NETHERLANDS

Cover picture:
This early 20th century card represents one view of the Cockhorse in the Banbury rhyme. It may well have been a hobby-horse in the fashion of a child's toy. Another explanation, perhaps hinted at here, is that since the roads out of Banbury have steep slopes on them an additional 'cockhorse' was needed to assist the coaches. Also suggested is that it refers to two people on one horse.

BACK IN TIME

GB ISBN 90 288 6374 5

© 1997 European Library – Zaltbommel/The Netherlands

No part of this book may be reproduced in any form, by print, photoprint, microfilm or any other means, without written permission from the publisher.

Introduction

In his introduction to the first volume of 'Banbury in old picture postcards', Ted Clark provides an outline history of the town and identifies some key dates in its development.
My choice of cards for this second volume has been determined partly by a desire to make a logical progression through the town and partly out of the need to highlight aspects of Banbury not previously considered.
The story unfolds in the Oxford Road and goes on to feature people, buildings and events. Two strong sub-themes concern the Cross at a variety of dates and its surroundings, and the part of Grimsbury immediately north of the Middleton Road. As in volume 1, the villages of Banburyshire are represented, and the book concludes with a delightful flight of fancy.

The dates 1880 and 1930 mark stages in the evolution of Banbury as a place to live and a place to work. In the final quarter of the 19th century ladies walked the promenade of the Oxford Road in their Sunday best, whereas by 1930 Banbury was sliding out of the Samuelson era of industrial prosperity based on engineering and was faced with a spell of urban obscurity.

Another and perhaps more traditional vision of the town was provided by the 1887 procession which was part of the celebrations for Queen Victoria's Golden Jubilee. The various floats gave expression to middle class commercial success and reminded those who turned out to watch that Banbury was a place of cakes and cloth and had been fired with Puritan zeal.
By the time of this procession Banbury was no longer just the hub of streets laid down past castle and market place. It included red light areas such as surrounded Calthorpe Street and came close to more desirable property in South Bar and the Green which consisted of splendid villas occupied by professional class people. Typical of these homes was Linden House, whose deeds remind us that gracious living could also include perks such as splendid pews in St. Mary's Church built in 1790.

This second volume of 'Banbury in old picture postcards' offers a further opportunity to relive days that have gone for ever as the town waits for further development that will project it beyond the Millennium.

The author wishes to thank the following for the use of their old picture postcards in this book: the Oxfordshire County Museum Service, Mrs. Kathleen Malcolm, Mrs. Gwen Killpack, Mrs. Rhoda Anker, Mr. Michael Jones and Mr. Archie Buzzard. Valuable information about some cards came from Mr. Barry Davis, Mr. Harry Colegrave and Messrs. Bill and John Stroud. Mrs. Christine Kelly (Banbury Museum Curator's Assistant) was helpful on numerous occasions.

Above all I am highly indebted to my wife, Mrs. Margaret Little, for hours of devotion to getting the captions word processed and for many constructive observations and suggestions.

1 An early 20th century postcard depiction of the Banbury Sun. A seal, of 1584, bears the device of a carved ornamental shield of arms, with the sun in splendour, and beneath it the legend SIGILLUM BURGI DE BANBURI DOMINUS NOBIS SOL & SCUTUM. The 'Sun' can be found on a number of buildings in the town including the Town Hall and former Corn Exchange (Midland Bank) at the top of the Market Place

2   The five key areas in the history of Banbury shown in about 1914: the Cross and St. Mary's; Cow Fair with its pre-1925 livestock market; Parsons Street for the Original Cake Shop and the sixteenth century Reindeer Inn; Marlborough Road with its church, centrepiece of the Wesleyan movement; and Broad Street heartland of Co-opville.

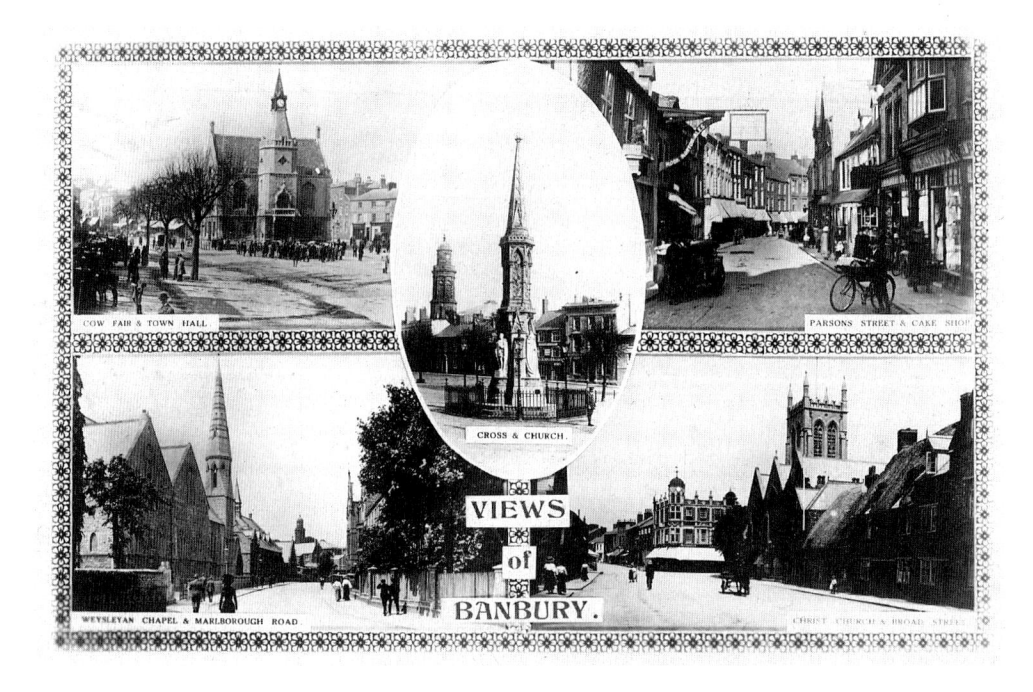

3   In the 1920s a lone trap passes the Oxford Road water tower, long since gone. Water pumped from Grimsbury by the Banbury Water Company was stored in a high service tank holding 50,000 gallons, thus enabling the company to supply a town expanding westwards.

4   The Oxford Road used to be home to professional class families living in their large villa properties. Prior to the erection of these properties this east side of the road consisted of four large fields called Windmill Fields, which formed part of the Calthorpe Estate sold in lots in 1833.

5 This card gives a clear view of the Promenade along the Oxford Road, where Victorian ladies walked on fine sunny Sundays. This raised pavement was the result of reducing the gradient of the road in 1839.

6   South Bar in the early years of this century. The South Bar gateway to the town used to span the road just above the Roman Catholic Church of St. John and close by Monument Street which was named after the obelisk erected in the late eighteenth century by Mr. Judd, a local carrier, who was allowed to take down the Bar which impeded the progress of his waggons. The obelisk marking the site was a condition of the Bar's removal, but did not survive beyond 1845.

7 South Bar and the Green assume the appearance of a fine tree-lined avenue in this Beale's photograph. The trees replaced an earlier avenue which had been planted in 1826 but later ruthlessly destroyed by a crowd led, we are told, by a maniac.

8   South Bar boasted a few shops including the photographic studios of Beale's (1888-1911). The lone cart on the right of the picture appears to belong to Dossett's, who ran a high-class grocery and wine merchant's business on the corner of North Bar/Parsons Street (Dossett's Corner).

9   Another Beale's view of South Bar includes the fine Georgian Linden House far left, which has had a long history of occupation from the early 18th century. Edward and Richard Barford acquired the property in that century and by its end the right to two pews in the new St. Mary's Church had been added to the lease.

10 A Valentine's shot of the Cross from West Bar Street early this century with, far right, the railings which bounded Linden House. A lease of 1787 notes that two tenements on the side of the house which flanked Bull Bar (West Bar) Street had been converted into one.

THE CROSS, BANBURY

11 This pre-1914 view of the Cross before the royal figures were placed in the niches indicates a reduction in the number of gas lamps that stood by the iron railings. Partly obscured by the trees is the run of Georgian properties facing the Green. In the 18th century this area was known as St. John's Street and was owned by the Bishop of Lincoln.

12 This card depicts a rhyme famous in Banbury history. Written by Richard Braithwaite in 1616 it pokes gentle fun at the extreme puritanism for which the town was known. By the time this rhyme was written Banbury had ceased to have a cross; the last remaining mediaeval cross became the target for puritan-inspired destruction in 1601.

THE PURITAN

To Banbury came I, O Profane One
Where I saw a Puritane One
Hanging of his Cat on Monday
For killing of a Mouse on Sunday.

13   The lady on a White Horse turns out for the peace celebrations of 1919. Local tradition has it that the reference to a 'fine lady' indicates that she must have been a member of the family of Lord Saye and Sele, whose ancestral home Broughton Castle is just outside Banbury. One of the family names is Fiennes (pronounced 'fines'). Others maintain that Banbury's most famous rhyme alludes to some folk memory of pre-Christian fertility rites.

Lady on White Horse, Banbury.

"Ride a Cock Horse to Banbury Cross,
To see a fine Lady ride on a White Horse;
Rings on her fingers and bells on her toes—
She shall have music wherever she goes."

14 Local photographers R. Brummitt and Sons have attracted a curious group. The scene reveals a large space between the Cross and the east side of Horse Fair, which was used for weekly sheep sales until marketing transferred to Midland Marts' Grimsbury site in 1925 or shortly afterwards.

The Cross, Banbury.

15 This impression of the Cross and Horse Fair around 1930 focuses on transport and includes a Phipps (Northampton) brewery dray (far right) standing outside the George and Dragon. The sheep market is no more, instead the space has become one of the best car parks in town. The iron railings around the Cross were removed in 1927.

16 Apart from sheep and horse sales, the Horse Fair was also a venue for meetings of the local hunts. By the 1930's no fewer than four hunts had Banbury as their centre. In addition to the Warwickshire Hunt seen here in 1909, there were the Bicester, Heythrop and Grafton. The building right background is a motor repair garage and advertises the sale of Pratt's motor spirit.

MEET OF WARWICKSHIRE HUNT JAN 15 .09.

17 The Horse Fair pictured from outside Church House looking back towards the Cross (just visible centre right) and St. John's Roman-Catholic church. The buildings on the right include the Three Tuns (now the Whately Hall Hotel).

18 A fine corner of the Horse Fair showing Church House (built 1905). Gone are the days when you could leave a barrow and barrel in the middle of the road leading to North Bar. This Beale's photograph also features the 16th century Friend's Meeting House (left of Church House).

19 This block formerly included the first ever Banbury premises of S.H. Jones, wine merchants. Many people were served by pony and trap. Early letters suggest that their custom was eagerly sought.

St. Mary's Church and Church House, Banbury

20 When Neithrop House and its grounds came on to the market, public subscriptions enabled a syndicate to purchase the estate. The grounds were then used as a public park under the syndicate. The park was opened in June 1912 by Mrs. J.W. Bloomfield, the then Mayoress, who planted a tree to commemorate the occasion.

SHADY WALK, THE PEOPLE'S PARK, BANBURY

21 A view of the People's Park showing the bandstand. In 1917 a deferred legacy from the will of Mr. G.V. Ball, a local chemist, enabled the Town Council to take over the park. It was officially opened as a public park by Lord North, High Steward of the Borough, as part of the peace celebrations in 1919. Between the wars hard tennis courts, a bowling green, a putting green, a children's playground and an aviary were added. The bandstand was the gift of a local body of trustees.

22 St. Mary's Church and vicarage around 1900. The present church is built of an attractive local marlstone and replaced a pre-1790 building of cathedral proportions. It was criticised by some people for lacking a steeple. This was remedied in 1822 when the tower was added.

23 St. Mary's Church just after the First World War. The iron gates have now gone, but the eighteenth-century church is still a symbol of local tourism and features on a poster at London's Marlebone station which advertises day trips to Banbury.

24 Southam Road and the cemetery gates. In 1854 the four burial grounds (those of the Parish Church, Roman Catholic Church, Baptist and Society of Friends) were closed and the cemetery in Southam Road opened.

25 The occasion was the Foresters' Procession of 1907. In the left foreground is the banner of a Bodicote group, closely followed by a Co-operative Society cart acting as a float. The event has attracted a good following, including some people watching from balconies.

26 Apart from the same procession, this picture tells us that nearby traders included W.M. Morgan, antique and furniture dealer, whilst at the junction of Fish Street (now George Street) there was Giles and Son, family butchers, whose promise was 'families waited upon daily'.

27   The butcher's business of Giles and Son began in 1899 and made a speciality of the 'noted Cambridge Sausage fresh daily'. Just a year later they were advertising in the official guide to a Fete held in the Dashwood Road grounds, July 1900. The cart proclaims telephone number 15.

28 S.H. Jones & Co, wine merchants, still occupy this sixteenth-century building, which was much altered in the early twentieth century when they took over the shop, following in the footsteps of an antique business and a bakery.

29 An unknown figure poses outside the side window of S.H. Jones which faces onto the entrance to Marlborough Road. The gas lamp with its bracket and the metal shop name plate have long since gone.

30 This door came from the original shop located in the Horse Fair. S.H. Jones traded from there until 1901, when the business moved to 62 High Street.

31   A flag-bedecked central High Street around 1910-1911, possibly marking the coronation of George V. Several prominent retailers can be recognised, notably Lipton's the grocers and K shoes. In the distance is the White Lion, Banbury's premier coaching inn.

32   A Boots own shot of the middle High Street in the early years of this century with their very striking sign. On the left is a window of the Red Lion.

33 An artist's impression of the courtyard of the Red Lion in the early years of this century. The Red Lion was located in the street of the same name (now High Street) and was the chosen venue for many local farmers, who ate there on market days and used it as a semi-official corn market. The premises extended through to Fish Street (George Street) where there was a tap facility. The Red Lion was pulled down in 1930 to make way for F.W. Woolworth 3d and 6d store.

THE COURTYARD, RED LION HOTEL, BANBURY.
The columns and capitals of the gateway of the Red Lion Hotel are of the 15th century perpendicular style of English Architecture, and appear to be the only remaining relics of a period so early as this within the town.—BEESLEY.

34 The eastern end of the High Street with A. Betts' cake shop occupying the 17th-century Edward Vivers building in the foreground. Cariers' carts are shown pulled up beside the shops, whilst their owners went in search of what their clients had requested. Sometimes this would include getting a prescription made up by a chemist.

CAKE SHOP, HIGH STREET, BANBURY.

35 A later view of the High Street. Blencowe and Son have taken over from A. Betts, but the Betts' name is still associated with the original Banbury Cakes for which the business was famous. Banbury Cakes were very popular in the world of railway catering. Arrivals at Banbury's G.W.R. station were greeted by a person with a tray of Banbury Cakes. Also noteworthy is the display of ironmongery outside Neale and Perkins.

36 Broad Street just before the First World War. The tower is that of Christ Church which opened in 1853 to serve the newly-created parish of South Banbury. To the left, the domed building of the Banbury and District Co-operative Society.

37 The Co-op building was opened in the summer of 1908 against a background of band music playing from the flat roof. This fine building was the hub of a business fast expanding in the Banbury area with a membership of over 3,000 people. The movement came to Banbury in 1866, when their sole building was a flimsy structure next to the Leathern Bottle in the Cow Fair.

38 Christmas time has always been a busy one for staff and pupils in primary schools. This costumed group is featured outside Britannia Road School in 1910, but not an infant in sight! It is likely that the group is the King's Messengers associated with Christ Church.

39 The Wesleyan Methodist Church was built in 1865 and was the third of a sequence of Wesleyan movement buildings including an earlier development in Church Lane. On his first visit to Banbury, William Mewburn of Halifax, who became an important benefactor, laid down one of the foundation stones.

40 A largely deserted Cow Fair shortly before the First World War. Along it and flanking the lower High Street are the stripy awnings of the shops which were the very core of the town's commerce. On the left-hand side railings held back animals on the days these were brought in for sale.

41 Cattle and carriers' carts bring life to the area east of the Town Hall. Doubtless some of the farmers in the picture have enjoyed a drink at one of the many inns and possibly also a market day shave and hair cut by the landlord of the Old George, who benefited to the tune of a few rabbits or pheasants.

THE COW FAIR, BANBURY.

42 Town Hall and Cow Fair in the early years of this century. Drovers brought animals into this thoroughfare from overnight pastures on the fringe of Banbury. On the northern side of the Cow Fair was a family shoe business called Cluff. It closed in the early 1960's and during a stock clearance the kinds of shoes farmers used on sheep as a guard against foot rot were found.

43 In 1931 the cattle market finally moved over the bridge to Midland Marts new saleyard and the area became the bus station for the ever expanding bus services to the neighbourhood. In this picture the crew pose by the side of their Midland Red service to Hook Norton, the driver in chauffeur's uniform. Curiously conductors had to make their own ticket racks by adapting mouse trap springs to appropriate wooden blocks. Behind the bus is Hunt Edmunds Leathern Bottle in the Cow Fair.

44 An unusual picture of a nearly deserted Market Place. In the 1920's and 1930's the twice-weekly produce market had some stalls which stayed open until 10.00 p.m. of a summer Thursday or Saturday. Shop owners often displayed their wares on the pavement and became a logical extension of the market activities.

45 An inter-war picture of the Market Place and Cornhill. In the foreground a solitary gas lamp such as illuminated the produce market area. In 1857 two rival Corn Exchanges had been built, one on Cornhill (right background with statue of Ceres and now the Vine entrance to the Castle Shopping Centre) and the other on the left which became Palace Theatre (Midland Bank), Banbury's first electric cinema which in its early days was owned by the Blinkhorn family. To the right the prominent corner building was occupied by Morlands, whose printing activities embraced a large collection of local postcards.

46 A Morlands' card of Parson's Street at the turn of the century. The Reindeer is a 16th century inn with later additions. Its first owners were members of the Knight family. The inn would have been popular with well-heeled travellers who used its parlour which was adorned with a globe. The narrowness of Parson's Street was a disadvantage to the Reindeer from the point of view of mail coach businesses. However, the S-shape which links the Market Place and North Bar was a major feature of town design.

Parson's Street, Banbury.

47 This postcard, date stamped 1915, has a message which sums up the myth that the Globe Room was taken to America. It was in fact found at a warehouse site in London and brought back to Banbury in the 1960's.

The Globe Room, Banbury

48 This early 20th century card shows a typical Civil War period trial scene. Folk history has it that Oliver Cromwell used to hold meetings in the Globe Room. Much later in Banbury's history, in the 19th century, William Mewburn (mentioned earlier in connection with the Wesleyan Church) met his team of builders in the Globe Room to plan the construction of Wykham Park, home today of Tudor Hall School.

Globe Room, Reindeer Inn

Banbury

49 A card depicting the two railway stations as they appeared soon after their opening. From the first, competition between the two railway companies was fierce. Bernhard Samuelson of the Britannia Works was a major customer of the G.W.R., but freight also used the line out of Merton Street (L.N.W.R.), though not always successfully. In one famous incident, a consignment of butter caught fire whilst on its way to London, due to sparks from the engine.

Great Western and London and North Western Railway Stations, Banbury, about 1854.

50   One man and his dog about to cross the River Cherwell in a punt. The river appears quite languid, but for centuries it has had the potential to flood seriously, especially in Spring. The Banbury Water Company selected the stretch about Fields Mill in Grimsbury as the best source for supplying the town.

51 The Middleton Road was the frontage to an area developed for housing in the late 19th century. The Banbury Freehold Land Society bought ground for housing in response to the town's growth of industry, and in particular the Britannia Works of the Cherwell Area.

52 West Street was cut northwards from the Middleton Road towards what in the early 19th century had been the start of the old Banbury Race Course. The first comers to West Street plots devoted their holdings to gardening, hence the name 'the Diggings'.

53 North Street. The Beale's photographer appears to have attracted many onlookers including children, who could use this street as a play area in comparative safety. Manure on the road suggests that horse-drawn carts came this way. Like other Grimsbury streets in the late 19th century, this one housed a proportion of industrial workers and their families.

54 Centre Street. Another Beale's photograph of a street in the same development. According to Barrie Trinder in 'Victorian Banbury' there were 25 houses in 1861 whose occupants included a postman, a millwright, a railway porter, a bricklayer, a boat builder and a coal wharf labourer.

55 South Street. In the 1860's some of the plot sites on the right-hand side were incorporated with properties facing the Middleton Road. Thereby they secured long gardens. On the left in the background is the Prince of Wales public house, which in the mid-19th century became the base for the earliest Banbury lodge established by the Foresters.

56 Daventry Road appears as a country lane in this early 20th century Beale's photograph. In the distance on the left is Huscote House, which was a part of a small farm typical of many in the Cherwell Valley. This stone property had been built on to the side of a barn and had a garden enclosed by a high wall. At different times it was in the ownership of a man named Wassell, who lived in South Street, Grimsbury, Maud Woodhull, who was well-known to Banburians as the owner of a number of properties throughout the town, and William Webb, who became a town councillor. It is likely that Maud Woodhull kept some livestock here.

57 Huscote Mill pictured here in the early years of the First World War was a very large red brick building concerned with grain. Residence here was affected by the Cherwell's propensity to flood, which meant that occupants like a family of Simpsons tended to inhabit only the top storey. The mill has been defunct long since.

58 Middleton Cheney Church. Like Bloxham, a notable feature is the church spire, which rises nearly 150 feet. However, it is the pre-Raphaelite glass which attracts so many visitors today. In the churchyard outside there are graves of Roundheads who died in the 1643 battle of Middleton. Also buried at Middleton Cheney is Miss Mary Jane Horton, whose desire to make a gift of a hospital to Banbury was generously carried out by her heir.

59 Middleton Cheney Co-op. The original Middleton Cheney store was trading from 1869. This Beale's photograph shows the opening of a new building in 1911 – part of a programme of expansion into the Banbury suburbs and surrounding villages such as Middleton.

60 Barley Mow. All lined up for the photograph outside the Barley Mow which stood on the western fringe of Banbury at the junction of the Warwick and Stratford roads. The message on the wall suggests that not everyone drank a little beer.

61 The Co-operative Society in Banbury developed an astonishing range of services and undertook deliveries of items such as bread and milk. Here the baker's cart is drawn up outside the Griffin Inn at Chipping Warden.

62 A Midland Red bus timetable of 1924 shows that Edgehill was a popular place for picnics and summer walks. The company ran charabancs which were well used. You could return to Banbury late evening after a pleasant time on the wooded slopes of Edge Hill.

Edgehill, near Banbury, (shewing a portion of the old ruins).

63 A somewhat artistic impression of Edgehill dating from the early years of this century. The battle of Edgehill, one of the many inconclusive 17th-century Civil War engagements, took place west of the scarp and resulted in huge loss of life.

64   Cropredy Bridge was another of the Civil War battles prior to the taking of Banbury Castle by Parliamentary forces. Like Edge Hill and many more minor skirmishes nothing was really settled. Waller was one of Cromwell's generals at Cropredy: recently his name has been adopted for a new housing estate in the lee of Banbury's Crouch Hill.

CROPREDY BRIDGE was the centre of the great battle, fought on June 2nd, 1644, between the Royal Army under Charles I. and the Parliamentary Troops. In the meadows adjoining, broken swords, cannon shot, and other relics have been found. It is situated 3½ miles from Banbury.

65 Bloxham Church is famous for its spire, 'Bloxham for length' says the rhyme. There was an earlier Norman building on this site, parts of which can be found in the chancel area. Restoration work took place in the 19th century and was carried out under the direction of G.E. Street, who also designed All Saints' School featured in postcard Nr. 74. Although sold by the Post Office Stores at Bloxham, this sepia card was printed in France.

BLOXHAM CHURCH

66   St. Peter's Church, Hook Norton, in the centre of the village. Its great height is emphasized by tall buttresses rising from ground level. The original Norman structure was transformed in the 15th century. Inside the church there are rare wall paintings and an enormous tub-shaped mediaeval font decorated with crude carvings of Adam and Eve and the Signs of the Zodiac.

St. Peter's Church, Hook Norton.

67 A tinted card in the Morland series. The heart of the old village nestles in the trees and in the distance high above the roof tops the tower of St. Peter's Church with its cluster of pinnacles dominates the village. Hook Norton is still home to a family brewery founded in 1849, which uses its own well water supply to produce the 'Hookey' ales, the village's best-known product.

68 Taken from Adderbury Green this card shows a fine sweep of stone-built cottages. Nearer the camera is the village pump, doubtless much used at the time this picture was taken in the early years of the century.

69 Rushers 19th century directories list 208 carriers who came to Banbury, often via several villages. As late as 1914 the figure was 118. One of the nearer of these was Plackett of Adderbury, whose carrier business was changed to an early bus connection.

70   Despite the sign board on the Midland Red bus, the village is Deddington. The bus is photographed in the square close by the imposing church which reflects Deddington's former importance as a thriving market town. The tower formerly supported a spire 'the most noted in all Oxfordshire' which fell down in 1634. It was rebuilt before the end of the century, strengthened with the buttresses which can be seen in the picture.

71   The stone cottages surround the Square at Aynho, seen here in a photograph of about 1910. Some of these buildings are amongst the most substantial properties in the village of that time and were occupied by the better-off members of an agricultural community.

72   An infant school was established in Cherwell Street in 1851. This was a response to the educational needs of the growing population of this area of Banbury. In 1861 the school transferred to Britannia Road premises, built with money provided by Bernhard Samuelson, who owned the Britannia Agricultural Engineering Company. At the time of this early 20th century photograph, Cherwell Infants' School would have had some 200 pupils.

73 Samuelson was again influential in the early development of education for older pupils. In 1893 his Banbury Municipal School was opened in Marlborough Road with 46 boys on the roll. Girls were first admitted in 1900. By 1928 numbers had risen to 270 and the building was overcrowded and unsuitable for such large numbers. In 1930 the County School, as it was now called, transferred to these fine new premises in Ruskin Road on the expanding Easington Estate, where there was provision for 360 pupils. This photograph has been dated to about 1931.

74 All Saints' School, Bloxham. Cricket has a long tradition in the public school world. In a history of All Saints' School published in 1978 there is a picture of a match in progress dated to 1863. A cricket XI appears to have been formed a year earlier, but the first serious matches were in 1863. This postcard shows the field soon after the turn of the century, a time made famous by H.B. Tordiffe, who made 211 out of 310 in one inter-dormitories match.

75 A fun card issued in the early days of flight and probably adapted to a range of locations throughout the country. The writer of the card postmarked 1912, has further adapted the caption to fit in with an invitation to stay in King's Sutton.

All the cards in this selection go a long way towards showing that the attractions of Banbury and Banburyshire are deeply embedded in its history.

Drop me in King's Sutton, Daddy.